JOHN BEZERRA

John Bezerra

Gen X's Path to Financial Freedom

THE SOCIAL MEDIA MONEY MACHINE

CONTENTS

| 1 |

Chapter 1: Introduction to Social Media for Gen X

The Rise of Social Media and Its Impact on Gen X

In the ever-evolving digital landscape, social media has emerged as a powerful tool that has revolutionized the way we communicate, connect, and do business. As Gen Xers, we have witnessed the rise of social media platforms like Facebook, Instagram, and Twitter, and have experienced firsthand the profound impact they have had on our lives. But what does this mean for us as adults aged 40-65 who are looking for a second income or to replace our existing income? How can social media help us achieve financial independence?

Social media for Gen X is not just about connecting with old friends or sharing photos of our vacations. It presents a unique opportunity for us to tap into the vast potential of the online world and leverage it to create a profitable income stream. Whether you're interested in affiliate marketing, e-commerce, content creation, or blogging, social media offers a multitude of avenues for us to explore and monetize.

Affiliate marketing on social media for Gen X is a lucrative and accessible way to generate income. By partnering with brands and promoting their products or services on platforms like Instagram or YouTube, we can earn a commission for every sale or lead that is generated through our unique affiliate link. With our years of experience and expertise, we possess the necessary skills to craft compelling content and build trust with our audience, making us highly effective affiliate marketers.

E-commerce on social media is another avenue that holds tremendous potential for Gen X entrepreneurs. With the rise of platforms like Facebook Marketplace and Instagram Shops, we can now easily set up online stores and reach a wide customer base. By leveraging our existing networks and utilizing effective marketing strategies, we can establish a successful e-commerce business and enjoy the freedom and flexibility that comes with being your own boss.

For Gen X bloggers, social media presents an invaluable opportunity to create and share content with a global audience. By developing a strong social media presence, we can attract a loyal following and monetize our blogs through sponsored posts, partnerships, and collaborations. With our unique perspectives and life experiences, we have the potential to create engaging and relatable content that resonates with our target audience.

Lastly, social media monetization strategies for Gen X content creators are essential to ensure that our efforts are financially rewarding. By diversifying our income streams and exploring avenues such as brand sponsorships, paid collaborations, and ad revenue, we can maximize our earning potential and achieve financial independence.

As Gen Xers, we have the advantage of both experience and adaptability. By harnessing the power of social media and leveraging our unique skills and knowledge, we can carve out a successful path to financial independence in the digital age. With dedication, creativity, and strategic planning, we can transform social media into a money-making machine that empowers us to live life on our own terms.

Why Gen X Should Embrace Social Media for Financial Independence

In today's digital age, social media has revolutionized the way we connect, communicate, and do business. While many Gen Xers may view social media as a platform primarily for millennials and Gen Z, it's time for the members of Generation X to realize the immense potential it holds for financial independence.

As adults between the ages of 40 and 65, you may be seeking a second income or looking to replace your existing income. Social media can be the key to unlocking a world of opportunities for you. Let's explore why Gen X should embrace social media for financial independence.

Firstly, social media offers a unique avenue for Gen Xers to make money online. Whether you have an existing business or are starting from scratch, utilizing social media platforms such as Facebook, Instagram, and LinkedIn can help you reach a wider audience and generate additional income. From promoting your products or services to leveraging affiliate marketing, social media can be your ticket to financial success.

Affiliate marketing on social media is particularly lucrative for Gen Xers. By partnering with reputable brands and promoting their products or services on your social media channels, you can earn a commission for every sale made through your referral link. This passive income stream can supplement your existing income or even replace it entirely.

Moreover, Gen X entrepreneurs can leverage e-commerce on social media to expand their reach and grow their businesses. With platforms like Shopify and Etsy, you can easily set up an online store and showcase your products to a global audience. By strategically utilizing social media marketing techniques, you can attract customers, drive sales, and increase your revenue.

For Gen Xers with a passion for writing or content creation, social media provides an excellent opportunity to monetize your skills. Whether you're a blogger or a content creator, platforms like YouTube, TikTok, and Medium allow you to showcase your expertise and build a loyal following. By implementing effective social media content creation and strategy, you can attract sponsors, advertisers, and even launch your own digital products or courses.

Lastly, social media monetization strategies are essential for Gen X content creators. By understanding the algorithms, engaging with your audience, and leveraging various monetization options such as sponsored content, brand partnerships, and crowdfunding, you can turn your passion into a profitable venture.

In conclusion, social media is not just for millennials and Gen Z. Gen Xers looking for a second income or to replace their existing income can benefit greatly from embracing social media. By exploring avenues such as affiliate marketing, e-commerce, content creation, and monetization strategies, you can pave your own path to financial independence. The time to harness the power of social media is now – don't let this opportunity pass you by.

Understanding the Social Media Landscape for Gen X

As a Generation Xer, you may have grown up without social media, but that doesn't mean you can't tap into its immense potential to generate a second income or even replace your existing one. In this subchapter, we will explore the various aspects of the social media landscape specifically tailored to Gen X, providing you with valuable insights and strategies to harness the power of social media for financial independence.

Social Media for Gen X: How to Make Money OnlineSocial media platforms have become virtual marketplaces bustling with opportunities for Gen X entrepreneurs. We will delve into the different social media platforms and discuss how you can leverage them to showcase your skills, products, or services. From Facebook to Instagram, we will guide you through the process of building an online presence, attracting an audience, and converting them into paying customers.

Affiliate Marketing on Social Media for Gen XAffiliate marketing is an excellent way for Gen Xers to earn passive income through social media. We will delve into the world of affiliate marketing, teaching you how to identify lucrative affiliate programs, create compelling content, and effectively promote products to your audience. Discover how to build trust with your followers while earning a commission for every sale made through your affiliate links.

E-commerce on Social Media for Gen X EntrepreneursIf you have dreams of starting your own online store, social media can be a game-changer. We will explore platforms like Shopify and WooCommerce, providing you with step-by-step instructions on setting up your e-commerce store. Learn how to optimize your social media profiles for sales, create engaging product descriptions, and implement effective marketing strategies to drive traffic and boost conversions.

Social Media Content Creation and Strategy for Gen X Bloggers Blogging has evolved into a highly profitable business, and Gen Xers have a wealth of knowledge and experience to share. We will help you develop a content creation strategy tailored to your niche, guiding you through the process of writing engaging blog posts, optimizing them for search engines, and promoting them effectively on social media. Learn how to attract a loyal following and monetize your blog through sponsored content, advertising, and more.

Social Media Monetization Strategies for Gen X Content Creators. If you're already creating content on social media, it's time to monetize your efforts. We will explore various monetization strategies, from sponsored posts and brand collaborations to selling digital products or courses. Discover how to negotiate fair partnerships, set reasonable pricing, and create a sustainable income stream from your content creation efforts.

By understanding the social media landscape and implementing the strategies outlined in this subchapter, you can unlock the full potential of social media to generate a second income or even transition into a full-time online business. Let's embark on this journey together and pave your path to financial independence through the power of social media.

| 2 |

Chapter 2: Building a Foundation for Success in Social Media

Identifying Your Passion and Expertise

In today's digital age, social media has become a powerful tool for individuals to not only connect with friends and family but also to create opportunities for financial independence. This subchapter will guide you, adults aged 40-65, who are looking for a second income or a way to replace your existing income, on how to identify your passion and expertise within the realm of social media. By harnessing the power of social media for Gen X, you can tap into various niches such as affiliate marketing, e-commerce, content creation, and monetization strategies.

First and foremost, it is essential to understand your passion. What topics or areas of interest do you feel most enthusiastic about? Is it fitness, cooking, fashion, or travel? Take some time to reflect on your hobbies, experiences, and knowledge base. By identifying your passion, you can align your expertise with social media platforms to create engaging content that resonates with your target audience.

Next, consider your expertise. What skills do you possess that can be valuable to others? Are you a seasoned marketer, a creative writer, or an expert in a specific industry? Leverage your expertise to establish yourself as a credible authority within your chosen niche. This will not only attract a loyal following but also open doors for potential collaborations and monetization opportunities.

For those interested in affiliate marketing on social media, it is crucial to find products or services that align with your passion and expertise. By promoting these products to your audience, you can earn a commission for each sale made through your referral link. This not only allows you to monetize your social media presence but also provides value to your followers by recommending products or services that you genuinely believe in.

If e-commerce is your preferred avenue, explore the possibilities of setting up an online store through social media platforms. Gen X entrepreneurs can leverage their passion and expertise to curate a unique product offering and reach a wider audience. Utilize social media marketing strategies to drive traffic to your store and convert followers into customers.

For Gen X bloggers, social media can serve as a platform to amplify your blog's reach and engage with a larger audience. Create a content strategy that aligns with your passion and expertise, and utilize social media platforms to distribute your blog posts. This can attract new readers, increase your blog's visibility, and potentially open avenues for sponsored partnerships or collaborations.

Lastly, social media monetization strategies for content creators involve exploring various revenue streams such as sponsored content, brand partnerships, and ad placements. By consistently creating high-quality and engaging content that resonates with your audience, you can attract brands and companies willing to invest in your platform. This can provide a substantial second income or even replace your existing income.

In conclusion, identifying your passion and expertise within the realm of social media is the first step towards financial independence as an adult aged 40-65. Whether you choose to venture into affiliate marketing, e-commerce, content creation, or monetization strategies, harnessing the power of social media for Gen X can unlock a world of opportunities. By aligning your passions with your expertise, you can create a lucrative second income or even transition into a full-time online business.

Setting Realistic Goals for Financial Independence

In today's digital age, social media has become a powerful tool for individuals seeking to achieve financial independence. This subchapter will guide adults aged 40-65 who are looking for a second income or hoping to replace their existing income through various avenues on social media. Whether you're interested in affiliate marketing, e-commerce, content creation, or monetization strategies, this section will help you set realistic goals to achieve financial independence.

When embarking on your journey towards financial independence, it is crucial to set clear and achievable goals. Without goals, it is easy to lose focus and become overwhelmed by the vast opportunities social media provides. By setting realistic goals, you can effectively chart your progress and stay motivated along the way.

Firstly, it's important to assess your current financial situation and determine how much income you need to achieve financial independence. This will act as a baseline for setting your goals. Consider your monthly expenses, savings, and any existing income streams. With this information, you can set a clear target for how much additional income you aim to generate through your social media efforts.

Next, it's essential to understand the niches within social media that align with your interests and expertise. Whether you're passionate about affiliate marketing, e-commerce, content creation, or blogging, identifying your niche will help you focus your efforts and maximize your chances of success. Each niche requires different strategies and approaches, so it's crucial to choose the one that resonates with you the most.

Once you've identified your niche, break down your financial goals into smaller, achievable milestones. For example, if you aim to generate $5,000 per month through affiliate marketing, you can set a milestone of reaching $1,000 within the first three months. These milestones not only make your goals more tangible but also allow you to track your progress and make adjustments if necessary.

Lastly, it's important to set a timeline for achieving your financial goals. This will help you stay disciplined and motivated throughout your journey. Consider factors such as the learning curve, trial and error, and the time it takes to build a solid online presence. It's important to be patient and understand that success may not happen overnight. However, with a clear timeline in place, you can stay focused and continually work towards your financial independence goals.

In conclusion, setting realistic goals is essential for adults aged 40-65 looking to achieve financial independence through social media. By assessing your current financial situation, identifying your niche, breaking down goals into achievable milestones, and setting a timeline, you can stay focused and motivated on your path towards financial freedom. Remember, success in social media monetization requires dedication, consistency, and adaptability, but with the right goals in place, you can turn your social media presence into a lucrative source of income.

Developing a Personal Brand on Social Media

In today's digital age, social media has become an essential tool for individuals looking to generate a second income or replace their existing income. For adults aged 40-65, also known as Gen X, leveraging social media platforms can unlock a world of opportunities for financial independence. This subchapter will guide you through the process of developing a personal brand on social media, enabling you to tap into various income streams and achieve your financial goals.

To start, it's crucial to understand the power of social media for Gen X individuals. With the right strategies, social media can serve as a platform for monetization, affiliate marketing, e-commerce, content creation, and blogging. By establishing a strong personal brand, you can position yourself as an authority in your niche and attract a loyal following.

The first step in developing your personal brand is to identify your target audience and niche. Consider your expertise, passions, and interests to determine the area in which you can provide valuable content and services. Once you have a clear focus, it's time to create engaging and high-quality content that resonates with your target audience. This could include blog posts, videos, infographics, or podcasts – whatever medium best suits your strengths and your audience's preferences.

Consistency is key in building a personal brand on social media. Regularly post content and interact with your audience to establish trust and credibility. Engage in conversations, respond to comments and messages promptly, and participate in relevant online communities. This will not only build your brand but also help you understand your audience better, allowing you to tailor your content and offerings to their needs.

In addition to content creation, it's essential to develop a monetization strategy that aligns with your personal brand. This could involve affiliate marketing, where you promote products or services and earn a commission for each sale made through your unique affiliate link. Alternatively, you can explore e-commerce opportunities by selling your own products or partnering with brands to create exclusive offerings.

As a Gen X individual, you have a wealth of life experience and expertise to share. By harnessing the power of social media, you can turn your knowledge into a profitable venture. With dedication, consistency, and an understanding of your audience, developing a personal brand on social media can pave the way to financial independence and a second income stream that complements or replaces your existing earnings.

Remember, building a personal brand takes time and effort, but with the right strategies tailored to your niche and target audience, you can leverage social media to maximize your earning potential.

Finding Your Target Audience on Social Media

In today's digital era, social media has become an invaluable tool for adults aged 40-65 who are looking for a second income or seeking to replace their existing income. With the advent of various platforms, such as Facebook, Instagram, Twitter, and LinkedIn, the opportunities for generating income online are abundant. However, to maximize your success in this arena, it is crucial to identify and connect with your target audience effectively.

For Gen X adults interested in using social media to make money online, understanding the nuances of each platform is essential. With the right knowledge and strategy, you can tap into the power of social media to boost your financial independence. This subchapter will guide you through the process of finding your target audience on social media and help you leverage your efforts effectively.

The first step in identifying your target audience is to define your niche. Whether you are interested in affiliate marketing, e-commerce, content creation, or monetizing your existing content, knowing your specialty will help you narrow down your audience. By focusing on a specific niche, you can tailor your content and marketing strategies to attract the right people.

Once you have identified your niche, it's time to dive into the social media platforms where your target audience spends their time. Each platform has its unique demographic, user behavior, and content format. By understanding these characteristics, you can optimize your presence on the platforms that align with your target audience.

Furthermore, social media analytics and insights are invaluable tools for understanding your audience. Utilize these features to gather data on your followers' demographics, interests, and online behaviors. This information will enable you to tailor your content and messaging to resonate with your target audience effectively.

Additionally, engaging with your audience is crucial for building a loyal following. Respond to comments, address concerns, and initiate conversations to foster a sense of community and trust. Regularly monitor and analyze the engagement metrics to gain insights into what resonates with your audience and make adjustments accordingly.

Lastly, collaborating with like-minded individuals in your niche can help expand your reach and tap into new segments of your target audience. By cross-promoting each other's content or products, you can leverage each other's networks and reach a broader audience.

In conclusion, finding your target audience on social media is a vital step in your journey towards financial independence. By defining your niche, understanding each platform's unique characteristics, utilizing analytics, engaging with your audience, and collaborating with others, you can effectively connect with your target audience and maximize your earning potential. Embrace the power of social media and unlock the opportunities it holds for Gen X adults seeking a second income or looking to replace their existing income.

| 3 |

Chapter 3: Leveraging Affiliate Marketing on Social Media for Gen X

What is Affiliate Marketing and How Does it Work?

Affiliate marketing has become an increasingly popular way to make money online, especially for adults aged 40-65 who are looking for a second income or want to replace their existing income. In this subchapter, we will explore the concept of affiliate marketing and how it can be effectively utilized on social media platforms, specifically targeting the Gen X audience.

Affiliate marketing is essentially a partnership between a company or brand and an individual, known as an affiliate, who promotes the company's products or services in exchange for a commission on any sales generated through their efforts. This form of marketing allows individuals to earn passive income by simply recommending products they genuinely believe in to their audience.

Social media has revolutionized the way we communicate and interact with one another, and it has also opened up new opportunities for online entrepreneurs. Gen X individuals, who have grown up with the internet but may not be as tech-savvy as younger generations, can leverage social media platforms to create an additional income stream through affiliate marketing.

E-commerce on social media is a thriving industry, and Gen X entrepreneurs can tap into this market by utilizing affiliate marketing strategies. By partnering with relevant brands and promoting their products on platforms like Facebook, Instagram, and Pinterest, Gen X entrepreneurs can earn a commission on every sale made through their affiliate links.

For Gen X bloggers, social media content creation and strategy are crucial for attracting an engaged audience. By incorporating affiliate marketing into their blogging efforts, they can recommend products or services to their readers and earn commissions on any purchases made through their affiliate links.

Additionally, content creators on social media can monetize their platforms by incorporating affiliate marketing into their strategies. Whether they are YouTubers, podcasters, or Instagram influencers, Gen X content creators can partner with brands and promote their products to their loyal followers in exchange for a commission.

In conclusion, affiliate marketing is a powerful tool for adults aged 40-65 who are seeking a second income or looking to replace their existing income. By harnessing the potential of social media platforms, Gen X individuals can effectively utilize affiliate marketing to generate passive income streams, whether through e-commerce, blogging, or content creation. With the right strategies and partnerships, affiliate marketing can become a lucrative endeavor for Gen Xers in their path to financial independence.

Choosing the Right Affiliate Marketing Programs for Gen X

In today's digital age, social media has become a powerful tool for Gen X adults looking to generate a second income or replace their existing income. With the right strategies and know-how, affiliate marketing on social media platforms can be a lucrative endeavor for this generation. However, with countless affiliate programs available, it's crucial to choose the right ones that align with the interests and values of Gen X adults. In this subchapter, we will explore the key factors to consider when selecting affiliate marketing programs for Gen X.

First and foremost, Gen X adults should focus on programs that cater to their niche interests. Whether it's health and wellness, personal finance, or lifestyle, finding affiliate programs that resonate with their passions will make marketing efforts more authentic and effective. By promoting products and services they genuinely believe in, Gen X adults can build trust and credibility with their audience, increasing the likelihood of generating sales.

Additionally, Gen X entrepreneurs looking to delve into e-commerce on social media should prioritize affiliate programs that offer high-quality products and exceptional customer service. This generation values reliability and long-term relationships, so partnering with reputable brands will not only boost their online reputation but also ensure customer satisfaction. Conducting thorough research on the program's track record, product reviews, and customer feedback will help Gen X adults make informed decisions.

Furthermore, social media content creation and strategy play a vital role in the success of affiliate marketing for Gen X bloggers. Choosing programs that provide valuable resources such as promotional materials, product images, and engaging content ideas can significantly streamline the content creation process. This support enables Gen X bloggers to focus on crafting compelling narratives and driving engagement, ultimately leading to higher conversions.

Lastly, monetization strategies are essential for Gen X content creators seeking to monetize their social media platforms. Affiliate programs that offer competitive commission rates, timely payouts, and transparent tracking systems are crucial for ensuring fair compensation. Gen X adults should prioritize programs that value their time and effort, providing them with the financial independence they desire.

In conclusion, choosing the right affiliate marketing programs for Gen X is paramount for adults aged 40-65 looking to generate a second income or replace their existing income. By focusing on niche interests, partnering with reputable brands, leveraging valuable resources, and prioritizing fair compensation, Gen X adults can pave their path to financial independence through social media. With the right strategies and dedication, affiliate marketing on social media can become a powerful money-making machine for this generation.

Creating Engaging Content to Promote Affiliate Products

In today's digital age, social media has become a powerful tool for individuals looking to generate a second income or replace their existing income. With the rise of social media platforms, adults aged 40-65, commonly known as Gen X, have a unique opportunity to tap into the vast potential of affiliate marketing and e-commerce. This subchapter will provide valuable insights and strategies on how to create engaging content that effectively promotes affiliate products on social media.

Social media for Gen X offers an incredible avenue to make money online. Affiliate marketing on social media allows individuals to earn a commission by promoting and selling other people's products. However, to succeed in this competitive landscape, it is crucial to create content that captivates your target audience and drives them towards making a purchase.

One of the first steps in creating engaging content is to identify your niche. Gen X entrepreneurs should focus on finding a specific market segment that aligns with their interests and expertise. This could range from health and wellness to home improvement or fashion. By narrowing down your niche, you can tailor your content to cater to a specific audience, thus increasing the chance of conversions.

Once you have identified your niche, it is essential to develop a content creation and strategy plan. This involves understanding your target audience and their pain points. Gen X bloggers and content creators should conduct thorough research to identify the needs and desires of their potential customers. By addressing their concerns and offering valuable solutions, you can establish yourself as an authority in your niche.

When creating content, it is crucial to strike a balance between promoting affiliate products and providing valuable information to your audience. Gen X content creators should aim to educate, entertain, and engage their followers. This can be achieved through various content formats, including blog posts, videos, podcasts, and social media posts.

To maximize the impact of your content, it is essential to leverage social media monetization strategies. This includes building a strong personal brand, engaging with your audience through comments and direct messages, and utilizing social media advertising and influencer collaborations.

In conclusion, creating engaging content to promote affiliate products on social media is an excellent opportunity for Gen X adults looking to generate a second income or replace their existing income. By identifying a niche, developing a content creation and strategy plan, and leveraging social media monetization strategies, Gen X entrepreneurs can unleash the power of social media to achieve financial independence.

Tracking and Analyzing Affiliate Marketing Performance

In today's digital age, social media has become a powerful tool for adults aged 40-65 who are looking to generate a second income or replace their existing income. With the rise of social media platforms, such as Facebook, Instagram, and YouTube, it has never been easier for Gen Xers to tap into the vast opportunities presented by affiliate marketing.

Affiliate marketing is a performance-based marketing strategy that allows individuals to earn a commission by promoting products or services on their social media platforms. It is a popular choice for Gen Xers because it requires minimal investment and can be done from the comfort of their own homes. However, to be successful in this field, it is imperative to track and analyze your affiliate marketing performance.

Tracking your affiliate marketing performance is essential to understand the effectiveness of your marketing efforts. By monitoring key metrics such as click-through rates, conversions, and sales, you can identify which strategies are working and which ones need improvement. This data-driven approach will enable you to optimize your campaigns, increase your earnings, and avoid wasting time and resources on ineffective tactics.

One effective way to track your affiliate marketing performance is by using specialized tracking software. These tools provide comprehensive analytics and reporting capabilities, allowing you to monitor the performance of your affiliate links across various platforms. They also offer advanced features such as split-testing, which enables you to compare different marketing strategies and identify the most profitable ones.

Analyzing your affiliate marketing performance goes hand in hand with tracking. Once you have collected enough data, it is crucial to analyze it to gain valuable insights into your audience's behavior and preferences. For example, by examining the demographics of your audience, you can tailor your content and promotions to better resonate with them. Additionally, analyzing your conversion rates can help you identify any bottlenecks in the sales process and make necessary adjustments to improve your results.

In conclusion, tracking and analyzing your affiliate marketing performance is crucial for adults aged 40-65 who are looking to make money online through social media. By using specialized tracking software and analyzing key metrics, you can optimize your marketing strategies, increase your earnings, and ultimately achieve financial independence. So, embrace the power of tracking and analysis, and watch your affiliate marketing efforts soar to new heights.

| 4 |

Chapter 4: Exploring E-commerce on Social Media for Gen X Entrepreneurs

The Benefits of Selling Products on Social Media

In today's digital age, social media has become an integral part of our lives. It is not just a platform for connecting with friends and family, but also a powerful tool for business growth and income generation. If you are an adult between the ages of 40-65 looking for a second income or to replace your existing income, selling products on social media can be a game-changer for you. This subchapter will explore the various benefits of leveraging social media platforms to sell products, specifically targeting Gen X individuals.

1. Wide Reach: Social media platforms like Facebook, Instagram, and Twitter have billions of active users. By selling products on these platforms, you can tap into a massive audience and potentially reach customers from all around the world. This wide reach increases your chances of making sales and expanding your customer base.

2. Low Cost: Unlike traditional brick-and-mortar businesses, selling products on social media requires minimal investment. You can start with a small inventory or even drop shipping, eliminating the need for upfront capital. Additionally, advertising on social media is cost-effective, allowing you to promote your products to a targeted audience without breaking the bank.

3. Increased Visibility: Social media platforms provide a level playing field for businesses of all sizes. As a Gen X entrepreneur, you can compete with larger companies by creating compelling content and engaging with your audience. By consistently sharing valuable information and showcasing your products, you can build a strong online presence, gain visibility, and establish yourself as an industry expert.

4. Personal Connection: Social media allows you to connect with your customers on a personal level. Gen X individuals value authenticity and genuine interactions. By leveraging social media, you can engage with your audience, respond to queries, and address concerns in real-time. Building these personal connections not only fosters customer loyalty but also increases the likelihood of repeat purchases and positive word-of-mouth referrals.

5. Data Analytics: Most social media platforms provide data analytics tools that enable you to track the performance of your posts, ads, and overall sales. By analyzing this data, you can gain valuable insights into your target audience's preferences, behavior, and purchasing patterns. This information allows you to refine your marketing strategies, optimize your product offerings, and ultimately increase your sales and profits.

In conclusion, social media platforms offer numerous benefits for Gen X individuals looking to generate a second income or replace their existing income. From reaching a wide audience and minimizing costs to building personal connections and leveraging data analytics, selling products on social media can be a lucrative venture. By adopting effective social media strategies and staying consistent in your efforts, you can harness the power of social media to create a successful online business and achieve financial independence.

Finding Profitable Products to Sell

In today's digital age, social media has become a powerful tool for generating income and financial independence. For adults between the ages of 40-65 who are looking for a second income or to replace their existing income, harnessing the potential of social media is a game-changer. This subchapter aims to guide Gen Xers through the process of finding profitable products to sell on social media platforms, enabling them to tap into the vast opportunities available online.

One of the most effective ways to monetize social media is through affiliate marketing. This strategy involves promoting products or services on your social media channels and earning a commission for each sale made through your unique referral link. Gen Xers can leverage their extensive knowledge and experience to identify products that would resonate with their target audience. By building a trustworthy relationship with their followers, Gen Xers can recommend products that align with their interests and needs, increasing the likelihood of conversions and earning potential.

E-commerce is another avenue that Gen X entrepreneurs can explore on social media. With platforms like Facebook Marketplace and Instagram Shopping, it has become easier than ever to set up online stores and sell products directly to consumers. By identifying niche markets and sourcing unique or in-demand products, Gen Xers can create profitable online businesses. Additionally, utilizing social media advertising and targeted marketing strategies can help attract the right customers and drive sales.

For Gen X bloggers and content creators, social media offers countless opportunities for monetization. By developing a strong content creation and strategy, Gen Xers can attract a dedicated following. Brands and businesses are constantly seeking collaborations and sponsored content opportunities with influencers, making it a lucrative venture. Gen Xers can leverage their expertise and knowledge to create valuable content that resonates with their audience, opening doors to partnerships, sponsored posts, and brand endorsements.

Furthermore, social media monetization strategies go beyond just promoting products. Gen Xers can explore avenues like creating and selling digital products such as e-books, courses, or templates. By identifying gaps in the market and leveraging their unique skills and experiences, Gen Xers can create valuable resources that cater to their target audience's needs.

In conclusion, the potential for financial independence and a second income through social media is immense for Gen Xers. By understanding the niches of social media for Gen X, affiliate marketing, e-commerce, content creation and strategy, and social media monetization strategies, Gen Xers can find profitable products to sell and pave their path to financial success. With the right approach, determination, and willingness to learn and adapt, the world of social media offers a wealth of opportunities for Gen Xers to thrive and achieve their financial goals.

Setting Up an E-commerce Store on Social Media Platforms

In today's digital age, social media has become a powerful tool for entrepreneurs looking to generate an additional income or even replace their existing one. For adults aged 40-65, who are looking for a second income or to replace their existing income, setting up an e-commerce store on social media platforms can be a game-changer. In this sub-chapter, we will explore the various aspects of leveraging social media for e-commerce, specifically targeted towards Gen X entrepreneurs.

Social media platforms like Facebook, Instagram, and Pinterest have evolved into more than just platforms for connecting with friends and sharing pictures. They have become virtual marketplaces where businesses can showcase and sell their products. As a Gen X entrepreneur, it is essential to understand the potential of these platforms and how to tap into them effectively.

The first step in setting up an e-commerce store on social media platforms is to choose the right platform for your niche. If you are targeting a younger audience, platforms like Instagram and TikTok might be more suitable. On the other hand, if your products cater to a more mature audience, Facebook and Pinterest could be better options. Understanding your target audience and their behavior on different platforms is crucial for success.

Once you have selected the right platform, it's time to create your e-commerce store. Most social media platforms offer built-in features for businesses to set up their stores. These features allow you to showcase your products, provide product descriptions, and even enable customers to make purchases directly on the platform. It is important to optimize your store for mobile devices as a significant portion of social media users access these platforms through their smartphones.

To drive traffic to your e-commerce store, you need to develop a robust social media content creation and strategy. Gen X bloggers and content creators can leverage their expertise and knowledge to create engaging and valuable content for their target audience. This could be in the form of blog posts, videos, or even live streams. By consistently providing valuable content, you can build trust and credibility with your audience, increasing the chances of them making a purchase from your e-commerce store.

Lastly, monetization strategies play a crucial role in generating revenue from your e-commerce store on social media platforms. Affiliate marketing is one such strategy that allows you to earn a commission for promoting other people's products. This can be a great way to supplement your income, especially if you have a loyal and engaged audience.

In conclusion, setting up an e-commerce store on social media platforms can be a lucrative venture for Gen X entrepreneurs looking for a second income or to replace their existing one. By understanding the potential of social media platforms, creating a compelling e-commerce store, developing a content creation and strategy, and implementing monetization strategies, you can tap into the immense opportunities that social media offers for e-commerce.

Promoting and Scaling Your E-commerce Business on Social Media

In today's digital age, social media has become an essential tool for promoting and scaling businesses. For adults aged 40-65 looking for a second income or to replace their existing income, harnessing the power of social media can open up a world of opportunities. In this subchapter, we will explore various strategies to help Gen X entrepreneurs leverage social media for their e-commerce ventures.

One of the most effective ways to make money online is through affiliate marketing on social media. As a Gen X entrepreneur, you can partner with brands and promote their products or services on your social media platforms. By strategically placing affiliate links and sharing valuable content, you can earn a commission for every sale made through your referral. We will delve into the best practices and techniques for successful affiliate marketing on social media, ensuring you maximize your earning potential.

E-commerce on social media is another lucrative avenue for Gen X entrepreneurs. Platforms like Facebook, Instagram, and Pinterest offer seamless integration with e-commerce functionalities, allowing you to set up your online store and sell products directly to your audience. We will guide you through the process of setting up an e-commerce store on social media and provide insights on how to drive traffic, increase sales, and build customer loyalty.

Effective content creation and strategy are key to success on social media. As a Gen X blogger, you can tap into your unique experiences and expertise to create engaging and relatable content for your target audience. We will explore different content formats, such as blog posts, videos, and infographics, and share strategies to create a consistent brand image and attract a loyal following.

Monetizing your social media presence is crucial for Gen X content creators. We will discuss various strategies, such as sponsored posts, brand collaborations, and creating digital products, that can help you turn your passion into a profitable venture. Additionally, we will provide tips on how to negotiate fair compensation and build long-term partnerships with brands.

In conclusion, social media has revolutionized the way businesses operate, and Gen X entrepreneurs can leverage its power to generate a second income or replace their existing one. By mastering affiliate marketing, e-commerce, content creation, and monetization strategies, you can create a successful online business while enjoying the freedom and flexibility that comes with it. Get ready to embark on a journey towards financial independence with the help of social media as your money-making machine.

| 5 |

Chapter 5: Social Media Content Creation and Strategy for Gen X Bloggers

Understanding the Importance of Quality Content on Social Media

In today's digital age, social media has become an integral part of our lives. It has transformed how we connect, communicate, and consume information. For adults aged 40-65 who are looking for a second income or to replace their existing income, social media presents a wealth of opportunities. Whether you are interested in affiliate marketing, e-commerce, blogging, or content creation, understanding the importance of quality content on social media is crucial for success.

Social media platforms, such as Facebook, Instagram, Twitter, and LinkedIn, offer a vast audience and the potential to reach millions of users. However, with this immense reach comes intense competition. To stand out and attract your target audience, you need to create quality content that resonates with them.

Quality content on social media goes beyond just posting random updates or sharing links. It involves crafting compelling and engaging content that provides value to your audience. This could be in the form of informative blog posts, visually appealing images and videos, thought-provoking captions, or entertaining stories. By consistently delivering high-quality content, you establish yourself as an authority in your niche and build trust with your audience.

For Gen Xers looking to make money online, affiliate marketing is an effective strategy. By promoting products or services through your social media channels, you can earn a commission for every sale made through your referral. However, simply bombarding your followers with affiliate links will not yield the desired results. Instead, focus on creating content that educates, inspires, or entertains your audience, while seamlessly incorporating your affiliate links.

E-commerce on social media is another avenue for Gen X entrepreneurs. Platforms like Instagram and Facebook offer built-in shopping features, allowing you to showcase and sell your products directly to your followers. To succeed in e-commerce, your content needs to showcase your products in the best light, highlight their benefits, and provide an easy purchasing experience for your customers.

If you are a Gen X blogger, social media is an excellent tool for promoting your content and driving traffic to your website. By developing a content creation and strategy specifically tailored for social media, you can effectively engage with your audience, expand your reach, and increase your blog's visibility. Consistency is key here, as regular posting and engagement will help you build a loyal following.

Finally, for content creators looking to monetize their social media presence, various strategies can be employed. These include sponsored posts, brand collaborations, product endorsements, and even creating your own digital products or online courses. However, to attract these opportunities, your content must be of the highest quality, align with your brand, and offer value to your audience.

In conclusion, social media has opened up a world of possibilities for adults aged 40-65 looking to generate a second income or replace their existing income. To succeed in this digital landscape, understanding the importance of quality content on social media is vital. By consistently delivering valuable and engaging content, you can attract your target audience, establish yourself as an authority, and ultimately achieve financial independence through social media.

Developing a Content Creation Plan for Gen X Bloggers

In today's digital age, it is crucial for Gen X bloggers to have a strong content creation plan in order to succeed in the online world. With social media becoming a powerful tool for making money and generating a second income, it is essential for adults aged 40-65 to understand how to effectively create and monetize content on various social media platforms.

The first step in developing a content creation plan is to identify your target audience and niche. As a Gen X blogger, you have a unique advantage of being able to relate to others in your age group. This allows you to create content that resonates with your audience and provides value to them. Whether your niche is social media for Gen X, affiliate marketing, e-commerce, or content creation, it is important to focus on a specific topic that you are knowledgeable and passionate about.

Once you have identified your niche, it is time to develop a content strategy. This involves creating a schedule for posting content and determining the type of content you will create. For example, if your niche is social media for Gen X, you may choose to create blog posts, videos, or podcasts that provide tips and strategies for making money online. Consistency is key when it comes to content creation, so it is important to stick to your schedule and regularly produce high-quality content.

In order to make money from your content, it is important to monetize it effectively. This can be done through various strategies such as affiliate marketing, sponsored posts, or selling your own products or services. For Gen X bloggers, affiliate marketing on social media can be a lucrative opportunity. By promoting products or services that are relevant to your audience, you can earn a commission for every sale made through your affiliate links.

Another important aspect of content creation is engagement with your audience. Building a community of loyal followers is essential for success as a Gen X blogger. Responding to comments, asking for feedback, and providing valuable content that sparks conversation are all effective ways to engage with your audience and build a strong online presence.

In conclusion, developing a content creation plan is essential for Gen X bloggers looking to make money online. By identifying your niche, creating a content strategy, effectively monetizing your content, and engaging with your audience, you can build a successful online business and achieve financial independence. With the right strategies and consistent effort, social media can become your money-making machine.

Optimizing Content for Social Media Platforms

In today's digital age, social media has become an integral part of our lives. It has not only revolutionized the way we connect with others but has also opened up a world of opportunities for individuals to earn a second income or even replace their existing income. This sub-chapter aims to provide adults aged 40-65, who are looking to tap into the power of social media for financial independence, with valuable insights on optimizing content for various social media platforms.

Social Media for Gen X: How to Make Money Online

For Gen X individuals, social media offers a plethora of opportunities to make money online. From freelance work to starting your own online business, the possibilities are endless. However, to effectively monetize your presence on social media, it is crucial to optimize your content. This involves understanding the unique features and algorithms of different platforms such as Facebook, Instagram, and LinkedIn.

Affiliate Marketing on Social Media for Gen X

Affiliate marketing is a popular way to earn money on social media. By promoting products or services and earning a commission for every sale made through your unique affiliate link, you can leverage your social media presence to generate income. To optimize your content for affiliate marketing, focus on creating engaging posts that seamlessly integrate the products or services you are promoting, while also providing genuine value to your audience.

E-commerce on Social Media for Gen X Entrepreneurs

For Gen X entrepreneurs, social media platforms provide an excellent opportunity to showcase and sell products directly to consumers. To optimize your content for e-commerce, it is essential to create visually appealing posts that highlight the unique features and benefits of your products. Utilize features like Instagram Shopping or Facebook Marketplace to make it easy for your audience to purchase directly from your social media profiles.

Social Media Content Creation and Strategy for Gen X Bloggers

If you're a Gen X blogger, social media can be a powerful tool to drive traffic to your website and grow your audience. To optimize your content for social media, focus on creating visually appealing and shareable posts that align with your blog's niche. Utilize relevant hashtags, engage with your audience through comments and direct messages, and leverage features like Instagram Stories or Facebook Live to provide unique and valuable content to your followers.

Social Media Monetization Strategies for Gen X Content Creators

As a Gen X content creator, your expertise and knowledge can be monetized through social media platforms. Whether you offer consulting services, online courses, or digital products, optimizing your content is crucial for attracting and converting your audience. Focus on creating informative and engaging posts that highlight your expertise while also providing tangible value to your followers. Utilize features like Instagram Guides or LinkedIn Articles to showcase your expertise and establish yourself as an authority in your niche.

In conclusion, optimizing content for social media platforms is essential for adults aged 40-65 who are looking for a second income or to replace their existing income. By understanding the unique features and algorithms of different platforms and tailoring your content to align with your goals, you can effectively monetize your social media presence and unlock the financial independence you desire.

Building an Engaged Community Around Your Blog

In today's digital era, social media has become an essential tool for individuals looking to generate a second income or replace their existing income. For adults aged 40-65, commonly known as Gen X, social media offers a plethora of opportunities to tap into the online market and build a successful online business. One of the key elements in achieving this success is building an engaged community around your blog.

A blog serves as the foundation for your online presence. It allows you to share your expertise, thoughts, and insights with your target audience. However, merely creating a blog is not enough. You need to foster a sense of community and engage with your readers to establish a loyal following that can potentially become your customers.

To begin building an engaged community, it's crucial to identify your target audience and understand their needs and interests. As a Gen Xer, you have a unique advantage of understanding the preferences and challenges of your fellow generation members. Tailor your content to resonate with this audience, addressing their pain points and providing valuable solutions.

Social media platforms offer an excellent opportunity to reach and engage with your target audience. Develop a comprehensive social media strategy that aligns with your blog's niche and objectives. Utilize platforms like Facebook, Instagram, Twitter, and LinkedIn to promote your blog posts, share relevant content, and interact with your followers.

In addition to sharing your own content, encourage user-generated content. Engage with your audience by asking questions, hosting polls, and requesting feedback. This not only makes your audience feel valued but also fosters a sense of community. Respond promptly to comments and messages, showing that you genuinely care about their opinions and experiences.

Collaborate with other Gen X bloggers or content creators in your niche. By cross-promoting each other's content, you can expand your reach and tap into each other's engaged communities. This can lead to increased visibility, new followers, and potential collaborations or partnerships.

Monetizing your blog and social media presence is the ultimate goal. Explore various monetization strategies such as affiliate marketing, e-commerce, and sponsored content. As a Gen Xer, leverage your expertise and credibility to create sponsored content or partner with brands that resonate with your audience.

Building an engaged community around your blog takes time and effort. Consistency is key. Post regularly, interact with your audience, and provide valuable content that keeps them coming back for more. By implementing these strategies, you can turn your blog into a thriving online business and achieve financial independence.

| **6** |

Chapter 6: Monetization Strategies for Gen X Content Creators on Social Media

Diversifying Your Income Streams as a Gen X Content Creator

In today's digital age, social media has become a powerful platform for individuals to express their creativity, share their knowledge, and connect with like-minded individuals. For Gen Xers, who may be looking for a second income or hoping to replace their existing income, becoming a content creator on social media can be a lucrative opportunity. However, relying solely on one income stream as a content creator can be risky. That's why it's essential for Gen X content creators to diversify their income streams in order to maximize their earnings and achieve financial independence.

One effective way to diversify your income as a Gen X content creator is through affiliate marketing on social media. By partnering with brands and promoting their products or services, you can earn a commission for every sale or lead generated through your unique affiliate links. This allows you to leverage your influence and monetize your content while providing value to your audience through trustworthy recommendations.

E-commerce is another avenue for Gen X entrepreneurs to explore on social media. With the rise of online shopping, setting up an online store and selling products directly to your followers can be a profitable venture. Whether you choose to sell physical products or digital goods, social media platforms offer a convenient way to showcase your offerings and drive traffic to your online store.

Social media content creation and strategy are crucial aspects of building a successful online presence. As a Gen X blogger, it's important to consistently create high-quality content that resonates with your target audience. By mastering the art of storytelling, crafting engaging captions, and utilizing multimedia formats, you can attract a loyal following and increase your chances of monetizing your content through sponsored posts, brand collaborations, and partnerships.

Lastly, Gen X content creators should explore various social media monetization strategies to diversify their income streams. From running advertisements on your videos or blog posts to creating and selling digital products such as online courses or e-books, there are numerous ways to monetize your content and generate passive income.

In conclusion, as a Gen X content creator, diversifying your income streams is essential for financial independence. By exploring avenues such as affiliate marketing, e-commerce, social media content creation and strategy, and various monetization strategies, you can maximize your earnings and create a sustainable income online. Remember, success in the digital world comes from adaptability, creativity, and a willingness to explore new opportunities.

Sponsored Content and Brand Collaborations on Social Media

In today's digital age, social media has become a powerful tool for individuals to not only connect with others but also to generate income. As an adult between the ages of 40-65, you may be looking for ways to supplement or replace your existing income. Social media presents a vast range of opportunities for you to explore, and one such avenue is through sponsored content and brand collaborations.

Sponsored content refers to posts or videos created by social media influencers or content creators in partnership with brands. These collaborations involve promoting products or services in exchange for compensation. For Gen Xers seeking financial independence, this can be an excellent way to earn a second income or even replace your existing one.

Affiliate marketing is another lucrative avenue for Gen Xers on social media. By becoming an affiliate, you can earn a commission for every sale made through your unique referral link. With your strong understanding of social media platforms, you can leverage your presence and engage your audience with persuasive content that drives them to make purchases.

If you're an entrepreneur in the Gen X demographic, e-commerce on social media can be a game-changer for your business. Platforms like Facebook, Instagram, and Pinterest offer built-in features that allow you to set up an online store, showcase your products, and reach a wider audience. By incorporating effective social media strategies, you can maximize your e-commerce success and increase your revenue streams.

For Gen X bloggers, social media content creation and strategy are essential to attracting a loyal following and monetizing your blog. By leveraging your expertise and experience, you can create valuable content that resonates with your target audience. Through strategic partnerships and collaborations with brands, you can generate additional income through sponsored posts, guest blogging, or product reviews.

Finally, as a content creator on social media, you have the opportunity to monetize your platform through various strategies. This can include sponsored content, brand partnerships, ad placements, or even offering premium content or services to your followers. By implementing effective monetization strategies, you can turn your passion for creating content into a sustainable source of income.

In conclusion, social media provides a wealth of opportunities for Gen Xers to generate a second income or replace their existing one. Whether through sponsored content, affiliate marketing, e-commerce, or content creation, there is immense potential to tap into the social media money machine. By understanding the unique needs and preferences of your target audience, you can create a successful online presence and achieve financial independence in the digital age.

Creating and Selling Digital Products for Gen X Audiences

In today's digital age, social media has become an essential tool for individuals looking to make money online. Generation X, those between the ages of 40 and 65, are no exception. With their experience and knowledge, they have a unique advantage in creating and selling digital products that cater specifically to their own generation.

One of the most effective ways for Gen X individuals to make money online is through affiliate marketing on social media. By partnering with companies that align with their values and interests, Gen X entrepreneurs can earn a commission for every sale that is made through their referral link. This allows them to leverage their social media presence and generate passive income while promoting products they believe in.

Another avenue for Gen X entrepreneurs is e-commerce on social media. With platforms like Facebook Marketplace and Instagram Shops, it has become easier than ever to set up an online store and reach a wide audience. By identifying the unique needs and preferences of their generation, Gen X entrepreneurs can create and sell products that resonate with their target audience, whether it be personalized home decor, nostalgic clothing, or wellness products tailored to their specific needs.

For Gen X bloggers and content creators, social media provides a platform to showcase their expertise and monetize their content. By developing a strong social media strategy that includes consistent and high-quality content, engaging with their audience, and leveraging various monetization strategies like sponsored posts, brand collaborations, and ad revenue, Gen X bloggers can turn their passion into a profitable second income.

Furthermore, Gen X individuals can create and sell digital products such as e-books, online courses, and webinars. With their wealth of knowledge and expertise in various fields, they can offer valuable content that helps their audience solve specific problems or gain new skills. By leveraging social media to promote and sell these digital products, Gen X individuals can tap into a lucrative market and generate a passive income stream.

In conclusion, social media offers a wealth of opportunities for Gen X individuals looking to make money online. By understanding the unique needs and preferences of their generation, utilizing affiliate marketing, e-commerce, and content creation strategies, and leveraging their expertise to create and sell digital products, Gen X entrepreneurs can achieve financial independence and secure a second income or replace their existing income. With the right strategies and dedication, Gen X can harness the power of social media to create their own path to financial success.

Leveraging Membership and Subscription Models on Social Media

In today's digital age, social media has become an integral part of our daily lives. From connecting with friends and family to sharing our thoughts and experiences, social media platforms offer endless opportunities. But did you know that social media can also be a powerful tool for generating a second income or even replacing your existing income? In this subchapter, we will explore how adults aged 40-65 can leverage membership and subscription models on social media to achieve financial independence.

Social Media for Gen X: How to Make Money Online

For Gen Xers looking to make money online, social media can be a goldmine of opportunities. By understanding the power of platforms like Facebook, Instagram, and Twitter, you can tap into a vast audience and monetize your online presence. Whether you're a seasoned social media user or just starting out, this subchapter will guide you through the process of building an online business and generating income through social media.

Affiliate Marketing on Social Media for Gen X

Affiliate marketing is a popular and effective way to earn money online, and social media platforms provide the perfect avenue for promoting affiliate products and earning commissions. This subchapter will delve into the world of affiliate marketing, providing step-by-step guidance on how to find the right affiliate programs, create engaging content, and drive traffic to your affiliate links. With the right strategies and consistent effort, you can turn your social media presence into a passive income stream.

E-commerce on Social Media for Gen X Entrepreneurs

If you're a Gen Xer with an entrepreneurial spirit, e-commerce on social media can be a game-changer. This subchapter will explore the various e-commerce platforms available on social media, such as Facebook Marketplace, Instagram Shopping, and Pinterest's Buyable Pins. We will also discuss how to set up an online store, source products, and effectively market your e-commerce business to reach your target audience.

Social Media Content Creation and Strategy for Gen X Bloggers

Blogging has become a popular way to share expertise, experiences, and insights with the world. For Gen Xers looking to monetize their blogs, social media plays a crucial role in driving traffic and engaging with readers. This subchapter will provide valuable tips on creating compelling content, developing a social media strategy, and leveraging platforms like Pinterest and LinkedIn to grow your blog's reach and generate income.

Social Media Monetization Strategies for Gen X Content Creators

From YouTube channels to podcasts, content creators have a multitude of options for monetizing their creations on social media. In this subchapter, we will explore various monetization strategies, such as sponsored content, brand partnerships, and paid memberships. We will also discuss the importance of building a loyal audience and maintaining authenticity to ensure long-term success as a content creator.

In conclusion, social media offers countless opportunities for adults aged 40-65 to generate a second income or replace their existing income. By leveraging membership and subscription models, exploring affiliate marketing and e-commerce, mastering content creation and strategy, and implementing effective monetization strategies, Gen Xers can tap into the power of social media and achieve financial independence.

| 7 |

Chapter 7: Growing Your Social Media Presence and Maximizing Engagement

Strategies for Increasing Followers and Engagement on Social Media

In today's digital age, social media has become a powerful tool for individuals looking to generate a second income or replace their existing income. This subchapter will explore effective strategies for increasing followers and engagement on social media, specifically tailored to adults aged 40-65 who are looking to make money online or grow their businesses.

1. Define Your Target Audience: To attract the right followers and engage with them effectively, it's essential to clearly define your target audience. Understand their interests, pain points, and preferences to create content that resonates with them.

2. Consistent Branding: Establish a consistent brand identity across all social media platforms. Use professional and visually appealing graphics, cohesive color schemes, and a consistent tone of voice to build brand recognition and trust.

3. Engaging Content: Create high-quality content that offers value to your target audience. Share informative blog posts, engaging videos, or entertaining podcasts that address their needs and interests. Use visuals, storytelling techniques, and relevant hashtags to increase engagement and reach.

4. Utilize Influencers: Collaborate with influencers who align with your brand and target audience. By leveraging their existing followers, you can increase your reach and credibility. Partner with influencers to create sponsored content, host giveaways, or cross-promote each other's products or services.

5. Run Contests and Giveaways: Organize contests and giveaways to encourage user participation and engagement. Require participants to follow your social media accounts, share your content, or tag friends to enter. This will help increase your followers and generate buzz around your brand.

6. Engage with Your Audience: Actively engage with your followers by responding to their comments, messages, and mentions. Show genuine interest in their opinions and build meaningful connections. This will foster loyalty and encourage your audience to share your content with others.

7. Collaborate with Like-minded Brands: Identify complementary brands or businesses within your niche and collaborate on joint ventures, such as co-hosting webinars, cross-promoting each other's products, or sharing content. This can help expand your reach and attract new followers.

8. Paid Advertising: Consider utilizing paid advertising options on social media platforms to reach a wider audience. Facebook, Instagram, and LinkedIn offer targeted advertising options that allow you to reach specific demographics and interests, ensuring your content reaches those most likely to engage with it.

By implementing these strategies, adults aged 40-65 can effectively increase their followers and engagement on social media. Whether you're a content creator, blogger, affiliate marketer, or e-commerce entrepreneur, these tactics will help you grow your online presence, attract a loyal audience, and ultimately achieve financial independence through social media.

Building Authentic Relationships with Your Audience

In today's digital age, social media has become a powerful tool for individuals looking to create a second income or replace their existing one. For adults aged 40-65, commonly known as Gen X, leveraging social media platforms can provide numerous opportunities for financial independence. However, to truly succeed in this realm, it is essential to build authentic relationships with your audience.

Social media for Gen X offers a plethora of possibilities, from affiliate marketing and e-commerce to content creation and monetization strategies. Regardless of the niche you choose, establishing genuine connections with your audience is the foundation for success.

When it comes to affiliate marketing on social media, building trust is crucial. Your audience needs to believe in the products or services you endorse. To achieve this, take the time to research and test the products before promoting them. Share your personal experiences and honest opinions, ensuring transparency and authenticity. Engaging with your audience through comments, messages, and live Q&A sessions will also help develop trust and credibility.

For Gen X entrepreneurs venturing into e-commerce on social media, building authentic relationships is equally important. Focus on understanding your target audience's needs and desires. Create content that is not only visually appealing but also informative and valuable. Respond to customer inquiries promptly and provide exceptional customer service. By building a reputation as a trustworthy and reliable source, you will attract repeat customers and generate positive word-of-mouth referrals.

For Gen X bloggers, social media content creation and strategy play a vital role in attracting and retaining an audience. Consistently provide high-quality content that resonates with your target demographic. Engage with your audience by responding to comments, asking for feedback, and encouraging conversations. By genuinely connecting with your readers, you will foster a sense of community and loyalty.

Lastly, for Gen X content creators looking to monetize their social media presence, developing authentic relationships is key. Focus on understanding your audience's interests and preferences. Tailor your content to their needs and engage with them regularly. Explore different monetization strategies, such as sponsored content, brand partnerships, or even creating and selling your products or services. By maintaining a genuine connection with your audience, you will have their support and loyalty as you grow your online business.

In conclusion, building authentic relationships with your audience is the cornerstone of success in the world of social media for Gen X. Regardless of your chosen niche, prioritize building trust, providing value, engaging with your audience, and staying true to your authentic self. By doing so, you will not only create a second income or replace your existing one but also foster long-term relationships and achieve financial independence.

Utilizing Social Media Advertising to Boost Your Reach

In today's digital age, social media has become an incredibly powerful tool for individuals looking to generate a second income or replace their existing income. With its vast reach and ability to target specific audiences, social media advertising has opened up new opportunities for Gen X adults to tap into the online marketplace.

This subchapter will explore various strategies and techniques for utilizing social media advertising to boost your reach and maximize your earning potential. Whether you're interested in affiliate marketing, e-commerce, content creation, or monetization strategies, social media can be your gateway to financial independence.

For Gen X adults looking to make money online, social media offers a wealth of opportunities. By understanding the different platforms and their unique features, you can effectively target your niche audience and drive traffic to your online ventures. Whether you're promoting products as an affiliate marketer or selling your own products through e-commerce, social media advertising can help you expand your business and increase your revenue.

Furthermore, this subchapter will delve into the importance of social media content creation and strategy for Gen X bloggers. With the right approach, you can create engaging and valuable content that resonates with your target audience, ultimately driving traffic to your blog and increasing your chances of monetization. From writing compelling articles to creating visually appealing images and videos, social media can be harnessed to amplify your message and grow your audience.

Lastly, we will explore various social media monetization strategies for Gen X content creators. Whether you're a blogger, vlogger, or influencer, social media platforms offer numerous opportunities to monetize your content through sponsored posts, brand collaborations, and advertising partnerships. By understanding the intricacies of these strategies and implementing them effectively, you can turn your passion into a lucrative income stream.

In conclusion, social media advertising is a game-changer for Gen X adults looking to achieve financial independence. By leveraging the power of social media, you can tap into a vast audience, expand your reach, and maximize your earning potential. This subchapter will equip you with the knowledge and tools needed to navigate the world of social media advertising and establish yourself as a successful online entrepreneur.

Analyzing and Adjusting Your Social Media Strategy for Optimal Results

In today's digital age, social media has become an essential tool for individuals looking to generate a second income or replace their existing income. For adults aged 40-65, also known as Gen X, social media can be a powerful platform to explore various opportunities such as affiliate marketing, e-commerce, blogging, and content creation.

Understanding the importance of analyzing and adjusting your social media strategy is crucial to achieving optimal results. Here, we will explore some key areas that Gen X individuals should focus on to maximize their social media success.

Firstly, it is important to understand your target audience and their preferences. As a Gen Xer, you may have a unique perspective and understanding of your peers' interests and needs. Utilize this knowledge to create relevant and engaging content that resonates with your audience. By analyzing the demographics and behavior of your target audience, you can tailor your social media strategy to effectively reach and engage with them.

Secondly, consider incorporating affiliate marketing into your social media strategy. Affiliate marketing allows you to earn a commission by promoting products or services through your social media channels. As a Gen Xer, you can leverage your experience and credibility to recommend products that align with your audience's interests. By carefully selecting affiliate partnerships and tracking your conversions, you can optimize your strategy to generate a steady income stream.

Additionally, Gen X entrepreneurs can utilize social media as a platform for e-commerce. With the rise of online shopping, there is a vast opportunity to create and sell products directly through social media channels. Analyze your target market's preferences and purchasing behavior to identify profitable niche products. By utilizing social media platforms' built-in shopping features and optimizing your content for conversions, you can turn your social media presence into a lucrative e-commerce business.

Furthermore, Gen X bloggers and content creators can benefit from analyzing their social media strategy to enhance their monetization efforts. By consistently producing high-quality and engaging content, you can attract a loyal following and increase your monetization opportunities. Consider diversifying your income streams by partnering with brands for sponsored content, offering premium subscriptions or courses, or utilizing advertising platforms.

In conclusion, for adults aged 40-65 looking to generate a second income or replace their existing income, it is crucial to analyze and adjust their social media strategy for optimal results. By understanding your target audience, incorporating affiliate marketing and e-commerce, and optimizing your content creation and monetization strategies, you can unlock the full potential of social media as a money-making machine. With dedication, consistency, and a strategic approach, Gen X individuals can pave their path to financial independence through social media.

| 8 |

Chapter 8: Overcoming Challenges and Maintaining Financial Independence

Overcoming Gen X's Technological Challenges on Social Media

In today's digital age, social media has become an essential tool for businesses and individuals alike to connect, engage, and monetize their online presence. However, for adults aged 40-65, commonly referred to as Gen X, navigating the constantly evolving world of social media can be a daunting task. This subchapter aims to address the technological challenges faced by Gen X individuals and provide effective strategies to overcome them, enabling them to tap into the vast potential of social media for financial independence.

One of the primary challenges faced by Gen X on social media is a lack of technical know-how. Many individuals in this age group may feel overwhelmed by the ever-changing landscape of platforms, algorithms, and digital marketing techniques. However, it is crucial to understand that age is not a barrier to success on social media. With the right mindset and a willingness to learn, Gen X individuals can leverage social media to their advantage.

To begin with, it is essential for Gen X individuals to familiarize themselves with the various social media platforms and their functionalities. This can be achieved through online tutorials, courses, or seeking guidance from younger family members or friends who are already proficient in using social media. By investing time in learning the basics, Gen X individuals can gain confidence in navigating these platforms and understanding their potential for generating income.

Another challenge faced by Gen X on social media is the concept of affiliate marketing and e-commerce. These strategies involve promoting products or services through social media platforms and earning a commission for every sale made through their referral. Gen X individuals can explore various affiliate marketing programs and e-commerce platforms that align with their interests and expertise. By carefully selecting products or services they genuinely believe in, they can build trust and credibility with their audience, thereby increasing their chances of earning a sustainable income.

Creating compelling and engaging content is another crucial aspect for Gen X individuals looking to make money online through blogging or content creation. This subchapter will provide insights into developing a content strategy tailored to the Gen X audience, taking into account their preferences and interests. It will emphasize the importance of authenticity and relevance in content creation, enabling Gen X bloggers to build a loyal following and attract potential monetization opportunities.

Lastly, this subchapter will delve into effective social media monetization strategies specifically designed for Gen X content creators. It will explore avenues such as sponsored content, brand collaborations, paid partnerships, and other income streams that Gen X individuals can leverage to monetize their online presence. By understanding the intricacies of these strategies, Gen X content creators can transform their passion into a sustainable source of income.

In conclusion, while Gen X individuals may face unique challenges on social media, their age should not be seen as a limitation. By embracing technology, investing time in learning, and adopting effective strategies, Gen X individuals can overcome these challenges and harness the power of social media to achieve financial independence. This subchapter aims to empower them with the necessary knowledge and tools to embark on their journey towards success in the digital world.

Balancing Personal and Professional Life as a Social Media Entrepreneur

As an adult between the ages of 40-65, you may be looking for a second income or even a way to replace your existing income. The rise of social media has opened up incredible opportunities for individuals like you to tap into the online world and generate income. However, it's essential to find a balance between your personal and professional life as a social media entrepreneur. In this subchapter, we will explore strategies and tips to help you maintain that equilibrium and thrive in your journey towards financial independence.

One of the first steps to balancing personal and professional life is setting clear boundaries. As a social media entrepreneur, it can be tempting to constantly be online, responding to comments and creating content. However, it's crucial to designate specific times for work and personal life. This helps you avoid burnout and ensures that you have quality time for yourself and your loved ones.

Another aspect of balancing personal and professional life is time management. With the flexibility that comes with being a social media entrepreneur, it's easy to get carried away or lose track of time. Creating a schedule and sticking to it can help you stay organized and focused. Prioritize tasks, delegate responsibilities if necessary, and set realistic goals to keep yourself on track.

Furthermore, self-care is paramount in maintaining a healthy balance. Taking care of your physical and mental well-being is crucial for long-term success. Make sure to incorporate exercise, healthy eating habits, and relaxation techniques into your daily routine. This will help you stay energized, focused, and ready to tackle the challenges of being an entrepreneur.

Additionally, it's essential to build a support network of like-minded individuals who understand the challenges and triumphs of being a social media entrepreneur. Joining online communities or networking with other Gen X entrepreneurs can provide valuable insights, guidance, and support. Lean on these connections for advice, accountability, and inspiration.

Lastly, don't forget to make time for personal interests and hobbies outside of your entrepreneurial endeavors. Engaging in activities that bring you joy and fulfillment will help you maintain a well-rounded life. It can also provide inspiration and fresh ideas for your social media content.

Balancing personal and professional life as a social media entrepreneur may seem challenging at first, but with dedication and intentionality, you can create a harmonious lifestyle. By setting boundaries, managing your time effectively, prioritizing self-care, building a support network, and nurturing personal interests, you can find success and fulfillment in both your personal and professional life. Embrace the opportunities that social media offers, and embark on your journey towards financial independence with confidence and balance.

Navigating Legal and Ethical Considerations in Social Media

In today's digital age, social media has become an indispensable tool for individuals and businesses alike. It offers a plethora of opportunities to generate income, build an online presence, and connect with a global audience. However, as you embark on your journey to financial independence through social media, it is crucial to understand and navigate the legal and ethical considerations that come with this territory.

First and foremost, it is essential to familiarize yourself with the legal aspects of social media. This includes understanding copyright laws, intellectual property rights, and privacy regulations. Using copyrighted material without permission or infringing on someone else's intellectual property can result in legal consequences. Additionally, you should be aware of the privacy settings and guidelines on various social media platforms to ensure you comply with the rules and protect your audience's information.

Ethical considerations are equally important when leveraging social media for financial gain. Honesty, transparency, and authenticity should be the pillars of your online presence. Avoid engaging in deceptive practices such as buying followers or posting fake reviews. Instead, focus on building genuine relationships with your audience, providing valuable content, and disclosing any sponsored or affiliate partnerships.

For Gen X individuals looking to make money online through affiliate marketing, e-commerce, or content creation, it is crucial to understand the Federal Trade Commission (FTC) guidelines. The FTC requires disclosure of any financial relationships or endorsements to maintain transparency with your audience. Failure to comply with these guidelines can lead to legal repercussions and damage your reputation.

Furthermore, as a Gen X blogger or content creator, developing a solid social media content strategy is key to success. This includes understanding your target audience, creating engaging and relevant content, and adhering to platform-specific guidelines. By consistently providing value and building a loyal following, you can establish yourself as an authority in your niche and attract monetization opportunities.

In conclusion, while social media presents tremendous opportunities for Gen X individuals seeking financial independence, it is crucial to navigate the legal and ethical considerations associated with this platform. By staying informed about copyright laws, privacy regulations, and FTC guidelines, you can protect yourself and your audience. Emphasizing honesty, transparency, and authenticity in your online presence will help you build a loyal following and establish a solid foundation for your social media monetization journey.

Staying Motivated and Focused on Your Financial Independence Journey

In the pursuit of financial independence, it is essential to stay motivated and focused on your goals. This subchapter aims to provide valuable insights and strategies to help adults aged 40-65 looking for a second income or to replace their existing income remain motivated and focused on their journey towards financial independence, specifically in the niches of social media for Gen X, affiliate marketing on social media, e-commerce on social media, content creation and strategy for Gen X bloggers, and social media monetization strategies for content creators.

1. Define Your Why: Start by understanding your underlying motivation for pursuing financial independence. Is it to have more time for family, travel, or pursue your passions? Identifying your why will keep you motivated during challenging times.

2. Set Clear Goals: Establish specific, measurable, attainable, relevant, and time-bound (SMART) goals for your financial independence journey. Break them down into smaller milestones to track your progress and celebrate achievements along the way.

3. Develop a Routine: Create a daily routine that incorporates activities aligned with your financial goals. Dedicate specific time slots for social media engagement, content creation, research, and learning. Consistency is key to success.

4. Surround Yourself with Like-Minded Individuals: Connect with others who are on a similar journey. Join online communities, forums, or social media groups focused on Gen X entrepreneurs, affiliate marketing, e-commerce, or content creation. Collaborate, share experiences, and learn from each other.

5. Continuously Educate Yourself: Stay updated with the latest trends, strategies, and tools in your chosen niche. Attend webinars, workshops, or online courses specifically tailored for Gen X individuals. Knowledge is power, and staying informed will give you a competitive edge.

6. Embrace Failure as a Learning Opportunity: Understand that setbacks and failures are a part of the journey towards financial independence. Learn from your mistakes, adapt your strategies, and keep moving forward. Remember, failure is not the end but rather an opportunity for growth.

7. Celebrate Milestones: Acknowledge and celebrate each milestone you achieve along your journey. Whether it's reaching a certain number of followers, making your first affiliate sale, or launching a successful e-commerce store, take the time to appreciate your progress and use it as motivation to reach the next level.

8. Take Care of Yourself: Self-care is crucial when pursuing financial independence. Prioritize your physical and mental well-being by maintaining a healthy lifestyle, practicing mindfulness, and taking breaks when needed. A balanced approach will help you stay motivated and focused in the long run.

By staying motivated and focused on your financial independence journey, you can maximize your potential and achieve your goals in the world of social media for Gen X, affiliate marketing, e-commerce, content creation, and social media monetization. Remember, it's not just about the destination but also about enjoying the journey towards financial freedom.

| 9 |

Chapter 9: Case Studies of Successful Gen X Social Media Entrepreneurs

Case Study 1: From Traditional Job to Social Media Success

In this chapter, we will explore the inspiring journey of John, a Gen Xer who was able to transition from a traditional job to becoming a social media success story. John's story serves as a testament to the power of social media for Gen X individuals who are looking to create a second income or replace their existing income.

Like many adults in the 40-65 age group, John found himself stuck in a monotonous 9-to-5 job that offered little fulfillment and financial security. However, he was determined to change his circumstances and explore new avenues for generating income. That's when he discovered the untapped potential of social media.

John began by educating himself on the various social media platforms and their potential for monetization. He quickly realized that he could leverage his existing skills and knowledge to create valuable content that would resonate with his target audience. With a deep understanding of affiliate marketing and e-commerce, John was able to identify profitable niches and create engaging content that appealed to his fellow Gen Xers.

Through consistent and strategic content creation, John gradually built a loyal following on social media. He established himself as an authority in his chosen niche, offering valuable insights and recommendations to his audience. As his influence grew, John started collaborating with brands and businesses that aligned with his values, becoming an affiliate marketer for their products and services.

But John didn't stop there. He saw the potential for creating his own e-commerce business on social media. With careful research and planning, he launched his own line of products catered specifically to the needs of his target audience. Leveraging his social media presence, he was able to drive traffic to his e-commerce store and generate a substantial income.

John's success didn't come overnight. It required dedication, perseverance, and a well-thought-out content strategy. He diligently analyzed the trends, engaged with his audience, and adapted his approach to stay relevant in the ever-evolving social media landscape.

This case study serves as an inspiration for Gen X individuals who are looking to tap into the power of social media to create a second income or even replace their existing income. By leveraging their skills, knowledge, and unique perspective, they too can embark on a similar journey towards financial independence. Whether it's through affiliate marketing, e-commerce, content creation, or monetization strategies, social media offers endless opportunities for Gen Xers to thrive and achieve their financial goals.

Case Study 2: Leveraging Niche Expertise for Financial Independence

In this case study, we will explore how Gen X individuals have successfully leveraged their niche expertise on social media platforms to achieve financial independence. Whether you are looking for a second income or hoping to replace your existing income, this case study will provide valuable insights and strategies to help you achieve your goals.

Social Media for Gen X: How to Make Money Online

Social media has become a powerful tool for individuals to earn money online. Gen X individuals, with their wealth of knowledge and experience, have found success in leveraging social media platforms to generate income. From building a personal brand to creating engaging content, this case study will provide step-by-step guidance on how to effectively use social media platforms to make money online.

Affiliate Marketing on Social Media for Gen X

Affiliate marketing is a popular way to earn passive income on social media. In this case study, we will explore how Gen X individuals have tapped into the potential of affiliate marketing to generate a second income stream. We will delve into strategies such as choosing the right affiliate programs, creating engaging content, and maximizing conversions to help you achieve financial independence.

E-commerce on Social Media for Gen X Entrepreneurs

The rise of e-commerce has opened up new opportunities for Gen X entrepreneurs. This case study will showcase how individuals have successfully built and scaled their e-commerce businesses using social media platforms. From setting up an online store to implementing effective marketing strategies, we will provide actionable insights to help you establish a profitable e-commerce venture.

Social Media Content Creation and Strategy for Gen X Bloggers

Blogging has become a popular way for Gen X individuals to share their expertise and monetize their passion. This case study will dive into the world of content creation and strategy for Gen X bloggers. From identifying your niche to developing a content calendar and optimizing your blog for social media, we will provide practical tips and techniques to help you create compelling content and attract a loyal audience.

Social Media Monetization Strategies for Gen X Content Creators

If you are a content creator, this case study will provide you with valuable insights on monetizing your social media presence. From sponsored content to brand collaborations, we will explore various ways Gen X individuals have successfully monetized their content on social media. Learn how to negotiate partnerships, set fair pricing, and create win-win collaborations that contribute to your financial independence.

In conclusion, this case study serves as a comprehensive guide for adults aged 40-65 who are looking to generate a second income or replace their existing income using social media. By leveraging niche expertise, adopting effective marketing strategies, and capitalizing on the power of social media platforms, Gen X individuals have paved their way to financial independence. With the insights and strategies provided in this case study, you too can embark on a path to financial freedom and secure a brighter future.

Case Study 3: Building a Thriving E-commerce Business on Social Media

In this case study, we will explore the incredible potential of building a thriving e-commerce business on social media, specifically tailored for Gen X entrepreneurs. Social media has revolutionized the way we do business, and with the right strategies and techniques, you too can leverage this powerful platform to generate a second income or even replace your existing income.

The Gen X generation, aged 40-65, has a unique advantage in the online business world. With years of experience and a deep understanding of their target audience, Gen X entrepreneurs can tap into their niche market and create successful e-commerce ventures.

One of the most effective methods to make money online is through affiliate marketing. By partnering with established brands and promoting their products on social media, Gen X individuals can earn a commission for every sale they generate. We will delve into the strategies and tactics that have proven successful for Gen X entrepreneurs in the affiliate marketing space.

Furthermore, we will explore the world of e-commerce on social media. With platforms like Instagram and Facebook, Gen X entrepreneurs can set up their own online stores and sell products directly to their audience. We will provide step-by-step guidance on how to set up an e-commerce business on social media, including choosing the right products, creating compelling content, and driving traffic to your online store.

For Gen X bloggers and content creators, social media offers endless opportunities for monetization. We will discuss effective content creation and strategy specifically tailored for Gen X bloggers, helping them build a loyal following and ultimately generate income through sponsored posts, brand collaborations, and advertising.

Lastly, we will reveal the most lucrative social media monetization strategies for Gen X content creators. From YouTube and TikTok to podcasting and live streaming, we will explore various platforms and how Gen X individuals can leverage their unique skills and experiences to monetize their content successfully.

By following the strategies and case studies outlined in this chapter, Gen X entrepreneurs can unlock the full potential of social media and create a thriving e-commerce business. Whether you are looking for a second income or to replace your existing income, social media offers a vast array of opportunities for financial independence. Embrace the power of social media and embark on your journey to financial freedom today.

Case Study 4: Monetizing a Blog and Creating a Digital Product Empire

In today's digital age, social media has become a powerful tool for individuals to create a second income or even replace their existing income. For adults aged 40-65, looking to explore new avenues for financial independence, harnessing the power of social media is a game-changer. In this case study, we will explore how Gen Xers can monetize their blogs and create a digital product empire.

Social media for Gen X has proven to be a lucrative platform for those who understand its potential. By leveraging affiliate marketing on social media, Gen Xers can tap into a vast network of potential customers and earn commissions for promoting products or services. This strategy allows them to generate income while sharing their passion and expertise with their audience.

Moreover, e-commerce on social media has become increasingly popular among Gen X entrepreneurs. With the rise of online marketplaces and platforms like Facebook Marketplace and Instagram Shopping, Gen Xers can easily set up their own online stores, showcasing their products to a broader audience. By utilizing effective social media marketing strategies, they can drive traffic to their online stores and increase sales, ultimately creating a sustainable income stream.

For Gen X bloggers, social media content creation and strategy are essential to attract and engage their target audience. By delivering valuable and engaging content, bloggers can build a loyal following and establish themselves as industry experts. This, in turn, opens up opportunities for sponsored collaborations, partnerships, and even the creation of their own digital products.

One of the most effective ways for Gen X content creators to monetize their online presence is by creating digital products. These can include e-books, online courses, or even membership sites. By packaging their knowledge and expertise into easily accessible digital formats, Gen Xers can create valuable resources that can be sold to their audience, generating a passive income stream.

To successfully monetize a blog and create a digital product empire, Gen Xers must adopt effective social media monetization strategies. This includes understanding their target audience, identifying monetization opportunities, and leveraging various social media platforms to maximize their reach and impact.

By following the strategies outlined in this case study, adults aged 40-65 can tap into the power of social media to create a second income or even replace their existing income. With the right knowledge, skills, and determination, Gen Xers can transform their online presence into a thriving digital product empire, providing them with the financial independence they desire.

| 10 |

Chapter 10: Conclusion and Next Steps

Recap of Key Takeaways and Lessons Learned

As adults between the ages of 40 and 65, many of us are looking for ways to either supplement our existing income or even replace it entirely. In the digital age, social media has emerged as a powerful tool that can help us achieve financial independence. In this subchapter, we will recap the key takeaways and lessons learned from "The Social Media Money Machine: Gen X's Path to Financial Independence," catering specifically to our target audience.

1. **Social Media for Gen X:** How to Make Money Online Social media platforms such as Facebook, Instagram, and LinkedIn have become lucrative avenues for generating income. By leveraging our existing networks and personal brands, we can tap into affiliate marketing, e-commerce, content creation, and more. The key takeaway here is to understand the unique characteristics and preferences of our target audience and tailor our strategies accordingly.

2. Affiliate Marketing on Social Media for Gen X Affiliate marketing is a fantastic way to earn passive income by promoting products or services on social media platforms. By partnering with reputable brands and creating valuable content, we can leverage our credibility and trust to drive sales and earn commissions. The lesson learned here is to focus on building authentic relationships with our audience and only promote products or services that align with their needs and interests.

3. E-commerce on Social Media for Gen X Entrepreneurs With the rise of e-commerce, social media platforms have become virtual marketplaces. Whether we have an existing business or want to start one, tapping into the vast potential of social media can help us reach a wider audience and increase sales. The key takeaway here is to invest time and effort in creating a compelling online store, optimizing product listings, and leveraging social media advertising to drive traffic and conversions.

4. Social Media Content Creation and Strategy for Gen X Bloggers Blogging has evolved significantly over the years, and social media plays a crucial role in expanding our reach and monetizing our content. By consistently creating valuable and engaging content, optimizing it for search engines, and promoting it effectively on social media, we can attract a loyal audience and potentially earn income through sponsored posts, advertising, or even launching our own digital products.

5. Social Media Monetization Strategies for Gen X Content Creators If we are passionate about creating content, whether it's videos, podcasts, or written articles, social media offers various monetization strategies. From sponsored content and brand partnerships to crowdfunding and selling merchandise, the possibilities are vast. The lesson learned here is to build a strong personal brand, engage with our audience, and explore different revenue streams to diversify our income.

In conclusion, social media presents an incredible opportunity for adults between the ages of 40 and 65 to generate a second income or replace their existing one. By understanding the key takeaways and lessons learned in this subchapter, we can harness the power of social media to achieve financial independence and create a brighter future for ourselves.

Developing Your Action Plan for Financial Independence on Social Media

In today's digital age, social media has become a powerful tool for individuals to generate income and achieve financial independence. This subchapter will guide adults aged 40-65 who are looking for a second income or wanting to replace their existing income on how to develop an action plan for financial independence using social media.

Social media for Gen X has immense potential for making money online. With the right strategies and knowledge, you can tap into this opportunity and unlock a new stream of income. One of the most effective ways to monetize your social media presence is through affiliate marketing. This subchapter will provide you with valuable insights and practical tips on how to leverage social media platforms to become a successful affiliate marketer.

Additionally, for Gen X entrepreneurs, e-commerce on social media is a game-changer. This subchapter will explore the various social media platforms and their unique features and functionalities that can help you establish and grow your e-commerce business. From creating compelling content to optimizing your social media strategy, you will learn how to maximize your online presence and reach a wider audience.

For Gen X bloggers, social media offers endless opportunities to monetize your content. This subchapter will delve into the world of social media content creation and strategy, equipping you with the knowledge to create engaging and shareable content that resonates with your target audience. You will also discover effective ways to grow your blog's reach and convert your followers into loyal readers and customers.

Lastly, this subchapter will provide valuable insights into social media monetization strategies specifically tailored for Gen X content creators. Whether you are a vlogger, podcaster, or influencer, you will learn how to leverage your social media presence to generate income through sponsored content, brand collaborations, and other monetization methods.

In conclusion, social media has opened up a whole new world of opportunities for adults aged 40-65 to achieve financial independence. By developing a well-thought-out action plan and implementing the strategies outlined in this subchapter, you can unlock the potential of social media for Gen X and pave your path to financial freedom.

Resources and Tools to Support Your Social Media Money Machine Journey

In this subchapter, we will explore the various resources and tools that can help you on your path to financial independence through social media. Whether you are looking for a second income or to replace your existing income, these resources will provide you with the necessary guidance and support to succeed in the digital world.

1. Social Media for Gen X: How to Make Money Online to kick-start your journey, it is important to understand the fundamentals of social media and how it can be leveraged to generate income. Books like "Social Media Marketing for Dummies" by Shiv Singh and Stephanie Diamond will provide you with a comprehensive overview of social media platforms and strategies.

2. Affiliate Marketing on Social Media for Gen X Affiliate marketing is a popular method to monetize your social media presence. Websites like ClickBank and ShareASale offer a wide range of affiliate programs that cater to different niches. "Affiliate Marketing: Secrets to Generating Online Income" by James J. Jones is a must-read for anyone looking to master affiliate marketing on social media.

3. E-commerce on Social Media for Gen X Entrepreneurs If you are an entrepreneur looking to sell products or services through social media, platforms like Shopify and WooCommerce can help you set up your online store seamlessly. "E-commerce Evolved: The Essential Playbook to Build, Grow & Scale a Successful E-commerce Business" by Tanner Larsson provides valuable insights into building a successful e-commerce business on social media.

4. Social Media Content Creation and Strategy for Gen X Bloggers Creating engaging content is crucial for building a loyal audience on social media. Tools like Canva and Adobe Spark offer user-friendly platforms to design eye-catching graphics and videos. Additionally, "Everybody Writes: Your Go-To Guide to Creating Ridiculously Good Content" by Ann Handley is a valuable resource for honing your content creation skills.

5. Social Media Monetization Strategies for Gen X Content Creators Once you've built a substantial following, it's time to monetize your content. Platforms like Patreon and Ko-fi allow you to receive direct support from your audience. "Crushing It!: How Great Entrepreneurs Build Their Business and Influence—and How You Can, Too" by Gary Vaynerchuk offers actionable insights on monetizing your social media presence effectively.

Remember, success in the social media money machine journey requires continuous learning and experimentation. Stay updated with the latest trends in the industry through blogs like Social Media Examiner and Neil Patel's website. Additionally, attending conferences and webinars hosted by experts in the field can provide you with valuable networking opportunities and insights.

By utilizing these resources and tools, you will be well on your way to achieving financial independence through social media. Good luck on your journey!

Embracing the Gen X Path to Financial Independence on Social Media

In today's digital age, social media has become a powerful tool for individuals seeking financial independence. And for Gen Xers, who are looking for a second income or to replace their existing income, social media presents a unique opportunity to tap into a world of online earning potential. This subchapter aims to guide Gen X adults, aged 40-65, on how to leverage social media platforms to achieve financial independence.

The first section of this subchapter delves into the realm of social media for Gen X, providing insights and strategies on how to make money online. By exploring various platforms such as Facebook, Instagram, and YouTube, Gen Xers will learn how to monetize their online presence through content creation, affiliate marketing, and e-commerce.

Affiliate marketing on social media is a proven path to success, and Gen Xers can capitalize on their experience and expertise to create a lucrative online income stream. This section will outline the steps to becoming a successful affiliate marketer on social media, including finding the right affiliate programs, building a loyal audience, and effectively promoting products or services.

Moreover, as Gen X entrepreneurs, social media offers a vast marketplace to showcase products and reach a wider audience. The subchapter will delve into the strategies and tactics for leveraging social media platforms for e-commerce success. From creating engaging content to utilizing targeted advertising, Gen X entrepreneurs will gain valuable insights on how to boost their online sales and expand their businesses.

For Gen X bloggers, social media content creation and strategy are paramount to building a successful online presence. This section will provide tips and tricks on curating compelling content, optimizing posts for maximum reach, and engaging with their audience for increased monetization opportunities.

Finally, this subchapter will explore various social media monetization strategies for Gen X content creators. From sponsored posts to brand partnerships and ad revenue, Gen Xers will learn how to leverage their online influence to generate income and build a sustainable online career.

In conclusion, social media has become a game-changer for Gen X adults seeking financial independence. By embracing the Gen X path to financial independence on social media, individuals aged 40-65 can unlock a world of opportunities in affiliate marketing, e-commerce, content creation, and monetization. This subchapter acts as a comprehensive guide for Gen Xers, providing them with the knowledge and tools needed to thrive in the digital landscape and achieve their financial goals.